New Directions
P.O. Box 80611,
Lansing, MI 48908

Become
a Pen Pal

GROWING UP IN OUR FATHER'S

FAMILY

**GROWING UP IN
OUR FATHER'S**

FAMILY

DAVE WILLIAMS

Growing Up In Our Father's Family

Copyright ©1982 by David R. Williams

Third Printing *(Revised)* 1998

ISBN   0-938020-11-0

Cover design by Joseph Oberlin.

Published by

DECAPOLIS
PUBLISHING

Printed in the United States of America

MHC   10 9 8 7 6 5 4 3 2

BOOKS BY DAVE WILLIAMS

Acknowledgements

I'd like to thank my terrific editorial team for their assistance in getting this project to press.

Eldon Langworthy
Linda Teagan
Glenda Rozeboom
Sue Heyboer
Sabrina Martinez

Thanks, Team!

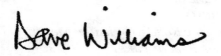

Contents

"But Jesus said, 'suffer little children and forbid them not, to come unto me: for of such is the kingdom of heaven.'"

— *Matthew 19:14*

Chapter 1

Introduction

Our Father has a family. Some members are on earth; some are in heaven.

For this cause I bow my knees unto the Father of our Lord Jesus Christ, of whom the whole family in heaven and earth is named. — *Ephesians 3:14-15*

God's family was created to bring joy to His heart — to give Him pleasure (Revelation 4:11) — and it always brings joy and pleasure to any father's heart when his children show signs of growth. When my daughter was two years old, she said to me one day, "Daddy, I love you a whole-whole-whole-*whole* bunch of a *whole bunch* of bunches!" That made me feel like a million! I realized that my little girl was growing up.

As children in God's family, we bring joy to our Heavenly Father's heart as we grow spiritually. Growing up in God's family means putting off child-*ish* characteristics, while retaining child-*like* characteristics.

The purpose of this book is threefold. First of all, we want to learn how to bring happiness and joy to our Heavenly Father's heart. Secondly, we will be able to zero in on how far we have grown spiritually. Finally, we will learn how to exercise patience with others who have not yet reached spiritual maturity. Also, it's important for us to understand that in certain areas of our lives, we may have grown in different phases. For example, a person may be very mature while facing trials, but very much a baby at getting along with others. That's why each of us must pinpoint our maturity level in the various areas of growth, then prayerfully allow the Holy Spirit to make the necessary changes (2 Corinthians 3:18).

Once a person is born spiritually, he or she becomes a newborn baby in Christ and the growing process begins. Advancement may come rapidly, or sluggishly. How fast a person grows depends on his or her own willingness to yield to the Word of God and to the Spirit of God.

Chapter 2

Babyhood Stage

The family of God is not an organization that can be joined. It's not like a club or a local church. The only way any person can be a part of it is to be *born into* it. That's what Jesus meant when He talked about being *born again*.

Jesus answered, Verily, verily I say unto thee, Except a man be born of water and of the Spirit, he cannot enter into the kingdom of God.

That which is born of the flesh is flesh; and that which is born of the Spirit is spirit.

Marvel not that I said unto thee, Ye must be BORN AGAIN.   *— John 3:5-7*

Obviously, no one is born completely mature. In fact, the opposite is true. When a person is born, he or she is known as an infant or a newborn baby. The Bible clearly refers to this stage of Christianity:

> As NEWBORN BABES, desire the sincere milk of the Word, that ye may grow thereby:— 1 Peter 2:2

> And I, brethren, could not speak unto you as unto spiritual, but as unto carnal, even as unto babes in Christ.

> I have fed you with milk, and not with meat: for hitherto ye were not able to bear it, neither yet now are ye able. — 1 Corinthians 3:1-2

Let's look at some of the characteristics of a baby and see if we can draw a spiritual parallel.

Characteristics Of A Baby

1. Babies are very dependent upon others. They can't feed or clothe themselves. They are completely defenseless. Someone else has to change them when they make a mess.

I once read an almost unbelievable news story about a demented mother who abandoned her newborn baby in the weeds along the side of an old highway. The poor little fellow couldn't defend himself, and insects began to gnaw on and sting his fragile, delicate body. All he could do was cry.

Several hours after the baby had been left to die, a driver heard his screams, stopped his car, and went searching for the baby. When he found the little boy, he was covered with insects. For several days after receiving medical attention, the baby teetered between life and death. Thank God, I'm happy to report that he lived and is well today.

Spiritually speaking, newborn Christians need someone to watch over them. Just as the little boy's mother left him helpless, older Christians commit a serious crime when they witness a "baby's" birth into God's family and then leave that infant alone and defenseless. It is too young to care for itself and needs the help and support of others. That is why a spiritual baby may call older Christians for help almost constantly, because he hasn't learned to feed himself yet.

Oh, spiritual babies may listen to tapes, attend revival meetings, conferences, and run to all the latest *spiritual restaurants,* but they haven't learned to feed from God's Word and discover His precious morsels of truth for themselves.

2. *Babies require constant supervision.* I remember a baby, just one year old, who got curious and pulled a pan of boiling water off the stove and onto himself. Today he is an adult and still bears the frightful scars. His mother took her eyes off him, and the accident happened.

Spiritual babies need supervision, too. There are dangers lurking: false prophets, false teachers, worldly attractions, enemy snares, etc. Remember, spiritual babies are like *lambs among wolves*.

3. *Everything goes into a baby's mouth.* Babies give everything the *taste test*. My daughter would eat soap, dirt, bugs, anything she could fit into her mouth. One time I caught her eating broken glass! My son went through this stage, too. His favorite treat was wax crayons.

Spiritual babies have a tendency to *taste test* every wind of *new* doctrine that blows around town. St. Paul had to contend with this in the early church. The Corinthians, being baby Christians, gave heed to dozens of ear-tickling heresies. The Galatians listened to the original Sabbath-day legalists, and the Colossians taste-tested some popular metaphysical teachings. Paul had to pull these poisonous substances out of their spiritual mouths in order to protect them.

4. Babies are jealous by nature. When I was 2½ years old, my mom brought my newborn brother home from the hospital. She was so proud of her new son. But what did I think? That was a different story. I looked him all over, and in a jealous-hearted style, stared angrily at mom and said, "Take him back!"

Spiritual babies, likewise, are jealous-hearted.

"Why does *she* get to be in the Easter Cantata and not me?"

"Why does *he* get all the good assignments from the pastor?"

"There must be a conspiracy. *He's* always elected to the best positions."

"Why did the pastor visit Mr. Doe? He never visits *me.*"

Spiritual babies!

Most Christians, however, do not remain babies. Most want to move on to deeper levels of maturity. In the following chapter we'll investigate the next phase of spiritual growth: *Childhood.*

Chapter 3

Childhood Stage

There is a transition between babyhood and adulthood. This transition phase is known as childhood. Childhood is a legitimate phase of growth, both naturally and spiritually.

> *That we henceforth be no more CHILDREN, tossed to and fro, and carried about with every wind of doctrine, by the sleight of men, and cunning craftiness, whereby they lie in wait to deceive;*
>
> *But speaking the truth in love, may GROW UP into him in all things, which is the head, even Christ:*
> — *Ephesians 4:14-15*

Let's take a look at some of the characteristics of a child.

1. Children are naturally curious, nosey, and snoopy. I'll never forget the day I discovered an interesting little hole in the backyard. I was three years old and very adventurous. *What could be in that hole,* I wondered. *Well, there's one way to find out,* I reasoned as I stuck my finger down the hole.

Suddenly it felt as though red hot pins were piercing into the end of my finger. I screamed hysterically as I jerked my finger out of that pinching bug's home.

But I didn't learn my lesson. Later, I found an old fuel oil tank and thought it would make a great space ship. So I crawled into it, not realizing that a colony of black wasps had made their home inside the tank. I suffered for my snoopiness again!

You'd think I would have learned, but not me! I found a ladder and realized I had never seen what was on top of the garage roof. So up I climbed, down I rolled, and off the roof I fell. It was a miracle I survived.

Curiosity can be a good quality if rightly directed. It can, however, be a dangerous quality when wrongly directed. I know a young Christian who ordered a cult magazine out of curiosity. He and his wife began to read it. I told him that the publishers were considered by evangelical Christians in general to be heretics, but he didn't listen to me. Now his life is one of misery after misery. He was once a joyous, soulwinning believer. Now he has a sadsack, run-of-the-mill type existence. Once he was a promoter of the Christian faith; now he discourages people from becoming involved in Christianity. All his misery started with a little misdirected curiosity.

2. *Children talk, talk, talk, talk ad infinitum.* A baby has become a child when the nonstop talking begins. Children talk almost constantly. The same is true spiritually. Spiritual children are usually gibber-jabbering about something or someone.

3. *Children are always trying to make an impression.* I took my kids to the park one day, and all the kids there gathered around to tell me or to show me what they could do. On the monkey bars, they each had to outdo the other. *Watch me! Watch me! I'm only six and I can beat up Johnny. He's eight. I can run faster than Tracy and he has longer legs!*

Children are always trying to outdo each other and impress people with their achievements. Likewise, spiritual children are always trying to impress someone. *I paid $20,000 for this car! Oh, look at my house! My sickness is worse than yours.*

4. *Children know it all.* This is especially true when children reach adolescence. They know more than mom and dad ... more than the teacher ... more than everybody!

When I was 13 years old, I asked my mother if I could back the car in and out of the driveway. She said no, but that my dad would take me to the park on Saturday. There he would teach me how to drive. But I couldn't wait that long. After all, driving is easy, I thought. *"R"* means reverse. *"D"* is for drive. What more did I need to know? So early the next morning I sneaked through the house, found the car keys, and headed for the driveway. *Nobody else will be up for another two hours or so,* I thought to myself.

Once I had started the engine, I put the transmission in *"R"*, and away I went ... straight into the side of the house. The house shook. Next I heard voices. Then came the footsteps — really heavy footsteps. My dad caught me and *rearranged my parts!*

As people mature, they realize how little they actually know. St. Paul, after 30 years of serving the Lord, said, "I count not myself to have apprehended." Paul never felt that he had arrived at the pinnacle of spiritual or educational knowledge. There is always room for growth.

Self-appointed, unteachable, Bible scholars are usually the ones who feel they've "arrived" and have no room left for any growth at all. But mature men and women of God realize how little they actually know.

5. *Children form cliques.* This is another indication of the adolescent phase of childhood. Spiritual children form cliques. Some groups say that ordinary Christians are outer-court Christians, while members of their clique are holy of holies Christians.

Another fad group says that ordinary Christians are just *children* of God, whereas members of their clique are *sons* of God. This kind of divisiveness is childish in God's eyes. (See 1 Corinthians 3:1-9)

6. *Children have a habit of fighting with their brothers and sisters.*

7. *Children are very unreliable.*

8. *Children are (generally speaking) undisciplined and unorganized in practical, everyday matters.*

Next, we'll take a look at *Maturity*, another phase of growing up in our Father's family.

Chapter 4

MATURITY

After babyhood comes childhood. After childhood comes maturity. For some people, this phase comes more swiftly than for others. Much depends upon the person. We'll look at principles of growth later in this chapter, but right now, let's take a look at some marks of maturity.

In Ephesians, God tells us that He gave the Church apostles, prophets, evangelists, and pastors/teachers with the intention of aiding in the believer's growth and maturity.

His intention was the perfecting and the full equipping of the saints (His consecrated people), (that they should do) the work of ministering toward building up Christ's body (the Church),

(That it might develop) until we all attain oneness in the faith and in the comprehension of the full and accu-

rate knowledge of the Son of God; that (we might ar-
rive) at really mature manhood — the completeness of
personality which is nothing less than the standard
height of Christ's own perfection — the measure of the
stature of the fullness of the Christ, and the complete-
ness found in Him.   — Ephesians 4:12-13 AMP

Verse 13 in the King James version reads, "unto
a perfect man." The word *perfect* comes from the
Greek word *telias* which correctly translated is,
mature! So, God is not looking for perfect people,
but *mature* people.

Yet when we are among the full-grown — spiritually
mature Christians who are ripe in understanding — we
do impart a (higher) wisdom (that is, the knowledge
of the divine plan previously hidden); but it is indeed
not a wisdom of this present age nor of this world or of
the leaders and rulers of this age, who are being
brought to nothing and are doomed to pass away.
*   — 1 Corinthians 2:6 AMP*

How does a person know when he's advanc-
ing into spiritual maturity? Let's look at some of
the obvious characteristics of a full-grown Christian, keeping in mind that all of us have room to
grow in some or many of these areas.

Qualities Of Christian Maturity And Growth In Grace *(Adapted from Charles Finney's exposition* Growth in Grace.*)*

1.   *A more implicit and universal trust in God.*

2.   *A separation from the world and an increasing deadness to all the world has to offer.*

3.   *Less temptation to sins of omission* (example: neglect of prayer, Bible reading, etc.).

4.   *A growing steadiness and intensity of zeal in promoting the cause of Christ.*

5.   *Less self-consciousness and more Jesus-consciousness.*

6.   *A growing deadness to the praise of men.*

7.   *A growing warmth and sincere acceptance of the whole will of God.*

8.   *A growing calmness and quietness under great afflictions.*

9.   *A growing patience under much provocation.*

10. *A joyfulness even when disappointments come.*

11.Less temptation to gripe, complain, criticize, and murmur.

12. Less temptation toward resentment and the attitude of retaliation when insulted, criticized or abused.

13. Less temptation to dwell upon and magnify our trials and troubles.

14. Less anxiety about the future.

15. Less inclination to speak uncharitably about another individual.

16. A growing readiness to forgive others and forget old injuries.

17. An increasing naturalness to treating people kindly and praying for them.

18. Finding it easier and easier to make wholehearted sacrifices.

19. We find ourselves more and more impressed with revelations of Bible truths.

20. A growing jealousy for the honor of God and for the honor and purity of His Church.

Now you should have a pretty good idea where you are, as far as spiritual growth is concerned; but you may be wondering, *How can I grow further?* There is a way to continuously grow in our Father's family. The key is threefold.

In the natural, a child grows by acquiring:

1. *Proper diet.*

2. *Proper exercise.*

3. *Proper rest.*

The same is true spiritually.

Proper Diet

Like newborn babies you should crave — thirst for, earnestly desire — the pure (unadulterated) spiritual milk, that by it you may be nurtured and grow into (completed) salvation. —1 Peter 2:2 AMP

The first key to spiritual growth is to desire spiritual food. The word *desire* literally means *to crave something.*

When I was a boy, growing up in Jackson, Michigan, my aunt took me swimming in

Vandercook Lake. Before she let me swim, she instructed me, "Now, David, don't go out into the deep water!" But I had to impress the girls. It was important for me to let them know that I was the 12-year-old swimming champ of the year. So, I swam out to the deep water, held my breath, went under the water and started turning around like a ferris wheel. I was doing somersaults in the water.

Well, all of my action stirred up clouds of dirt, and by the time I realized I needed to surface for air, I couldn't tell which way was up. I started kicking, and fighting, and was frantically trying to swim to the top when my head hit the bottom of the lake. By that time, I was *craving* a breath of air like I had never craved anything in my life. Thank God, I made it to the surface and survived, but the point is this: *I craved that breath of air.* When we begin to crave spiritual things, such as Bible reading and study, as much as a drowning person craves a breath of air, then we are on the pathway to growth.

How do we develop a craving for spiritual things? Human beings were created as creatures of habit, and studies have determined that in most humans a habit is established in 21 days. In other words, if you eat a chocolate bar every day for 21 days, on the 22nd day you would literally *crave* a chocolate bar. People develop habits whether consciously or unconsciously. We have literal cravings!

This information can go to work for you when it comes to your spiritual life. For example, if you can discipline yourself to get up a half hour earlier for 21 days and use that extra time to read the Bible, on the 22nd day you will literally crave God's Word. Once you've established an ingrained habit, you will actually crave the Word of God. In fact, you'll crave it so much that you'll wonder if you can make it through a day without it. (Imagine that: A Bible addict!)

God's Word can change your thinking, change your outlook, and change your life from defeat to victory, from failure to success. It's the Word of God that will acquaint you with the Father in an intimate way. It's the Word that will expose the enemy's tactics and methods. It's the Word that will reveal all of your assets in Christ. It's the Word that will give guidance and light to your path. What's wrong with craving God's Word? Nothing! Do it for 21 days, if you don't already. Systematically read the New Testament as much as you can.

Proper Exercise

> *Then we will no longer be infants, tossed back and forth by the waves, and blown here and there by every wind of teaching and by the cunning and craftiness of men in their deceitful scheming.*
>
> *Instead, speaking the truth in love, we will in all things GROW UP into Him who is the Head, that is, Christ.*
>
> *From Him the whole body, joined and held together by every supporting ligament, GROWS AND BUILDS ITSELF UP in love, as each part does its work.*
> *— Ephesians 4:14-16 NIV*

Begin right now to look for opportunities to reach out and exercise.

Exercise your faith. When you see a promise for you in God's Word, claim it and don't let go until it becomes a reality.

Exercise your service. Reach out beyond yourself and serve others. Take nursery duty. Offer to help on building and expansion programs. Look for ways to unselfishly serve others. One cannot grow apart from this practice.

Exercise your testimony. Tell someone, preferably a non-Christian, what Jesus has done for you.

Growth occurs with proper diet, proper exercise, and one other thing — *proper rest!*

Proper Rest

Proper rest is essential to healthy growth. Spiritually speaking, in order to experience proper growth, we must learn to rest in Jesus. Some folks are always struggling to be accepted by God. They struggle and toil to be righteous, not realizing that true righteousness, acceptance by God, comes only through trusting in the fact that Jesus has already clothed them with His righteousness when they received Him as Savior. The moment a person becomes a Christian, he or she is 100% righteous in God's sight. Nothing can be added to it to make it any better. Learn to rest in God. Rest in the fact that God is for you, not against you.

There remaineth therefore a rest to the people of God.

For he that is entered into his rest, he also hath ceased from his own works, as God did from His.
— Hebrews 4:9-10

Come unto me, all ye that labor and are heavy laden, and I will give you rest. — *Matthew 11:28*

Do you want to grow up in our Father's family?

1. *Crave the proper diet.*

2. *Get regular exercise.*

3. *Rest in our Lord Jesus Christ!*

Chapter 5

The Master Key To Greatness

There is a master key to greatness. Jesus spoke of it often (see Matthew 18:1-6, Luke 9:46-48; 22:24-27, Mark 10:35-45, and Galatians 5:13-15). He told of the Father's plan for our greatness, and He explained what we must do to attain it.

And He came to Capernaum: and being in the house He asked them, What was it that ye disputed among yourselves by the way?

But they held their peace: for by the way they had disputed among themselves, who should be the greatest.

And He sat down, and called the twelve, and saith unto them, If any man desire to be first, the same shall be last of all, and servant of all. — Mark 9:33-35

Nothing can destroy a ministry or a spiritual life faster than a self-seeking desire for power and prestige, but Jesus never rebuked the disciples' basic *desire* for greatness. He simply told them they could not become genuinely great without first becoming a servant.

> *But Jesus called them to him, and saith unto them, Ye know that they which are accounted to rule over the Gentiles exercise lordship over them; and their great ones exercise authority upon them.*
>
> *But so shall it not be among you: but whosoever will be great among you, shall be your minister: And whosoever of you will be the chiefest, shall be servant of all.*
> — *Mark 10:43-44*

Do you desire greatness? Do you desire to have a great ministry, a great business, a great marriage? The key then is this: ***Become service-minded and servant-hearted***

Tea Company

The president of a famous tea company was interviewed on a television program a few years ago. At that time, he was only 32 years old and was considered to be the hero of the business world; a multi-millionaire. When asked if he had any heroes of his own and what was the secret of his rapid success, he replied, "Jesus Christ is my greatest hero. He's my Lord. And Jesus gave us principles for success. One of those principles is to become a servant. I made myself and my company the servant of the public. We constantly looked for better ways to produce the best, the healthiest, and the tastiest tea ever." God honored His principle of greatness from there.

The best and most profitable gas stations are the ones that offer the best *service*. The greatest manufacturers in the world are the ones that provide top-notch *service*, even after the sale.

When I appoint leaders to specific positions in our church, I look for three basic qualities:

1. Does this person have a servant's heart or does this person merely seek the prestige of a position? What motivates this person?

2. Is this person teachable? Some people go through the same trials year-after-year because they have never allowed themselves to learn from God, from others, and from past experiences.

3. Does this person have an ever-increasing desire to draw closer to Jesus?

Leadership can be taught if these three attitudes are present: servant-heartedness, teachableness, and a desire to draw closer to the Lord.

The Measure Of Greatness

Greatness is measured by a person's unselfish willingness to serve, even in the seemingly small areas of life.

Ministry

The greatest churches and ministries are those that serve unselfishly. If people are coming to church, and the church is growing, it is because people are being served. They are receiving the spiritual nourishment they need and desire.

A youth ministry which was part of a California church decided they needed to reach out and serve if they were ever to become a great youth ministry. So they prayerfully sought the Lord for an idea, and He gave them one! They were to offer their services to widows, shut-ins, and elderly people in the community who needed help in everyday chores. They washed clothes, weeded gardens, washed windows, mowed lawns, and did other odd jobs. Often people would give them offerings for their services, although they didn't set any specific price on anything they did.

The youth department's enthusiasm began to explode! They had fun serving the Lord by serving other people. Soon revival broke out among the youth and then spread over to the adults. Today that church has over 35,000 people meeting weekly for worship and Bible study!

Great ministries are *service-minded.*

Business

Harvey is a salesman and so is Elmer. Both are Christians, but Elmer gets 500% more business than Harvey. Elmer also earns 500% more annual salary than Harvey. Why? Because Elmer is service-minded and Harvey is selfish-minded.

Elmer's attitude is, "I'm here to help the customer in any way I can. I am the customer's servant."

Harvey's attitude is, "I'm out to make a sale by hook or by crook. I've got to support my family, you know!"

Service-minded business people will always win in the long run.

Families

I know of a lady who received new strength and joy when she took action to serve her husband breakfast every morning. It was difficult for her at first, because she hadn't done it in such a long time. She was always too tired to get up that early. But when she made the decision to *serve* and started doing it, God opened some wonderful doors of opportunity for her to minister to women outside her home.

Can you imagine what would happen if all employees viewed themselves as servants to their employers and all employers viewed themselves as servants of the employees? There would be no more costly labor/management disputes. Industrial productivity would skyrocket and America would be back on the road to economic greatness!

It's fun and rewarding to be service-minded. You'll find yourself beginning to search for practical ways of serving, and you'll find that God will begin to reward you with greatness.

How To Serve

How should Christians serve?

1. Serve in a way that does not draw attention to yourself. (See Matthew 6:1-4.) Some people do a good deed and then broadcast it for the next three months. Don't sound the trumpet when you serve. Otherwise, you will have no reward of greatness. If you serve in a way that does not seek credit or recognition of man, God will reward you openly.

2. Serve in a way that you can. Nobody can serve in *every* capacity, but everybody can serve in *some* capacity. With maturity, recognize your limitations and look for opportunities to serve in ways that you can.

While building a new addition to our church, a roof expert told us that he and his crew would gladly do the roofing. He was looking for the opportunity to serve in a way that he could. It would not have been wise for him to say, "I'd love to try my luck at putting in the plumbing." His field of expertise was roofing, not plumbing. Each of us should serve in a way that we can.

3. Serve faithfully. If you will be faithful (reliable and dependable) in the smaller things, God will give you charge over greater things.

His master said to him, Well done, you upright (honorable, admirable) and faithful servant! You have been faithful and trustworthy over a little; I will put you in charge of much. Enter into and share the joy — the delight, the blessedness — which your master enjoys.
— Matthew 25:21 AMP

Becoming service-minded and servant-hearted is a necessary step in growing up in our Father's family.

Chapter 6

Listening And Learning

The art of listening is an essential element in the process of discipleship and growing up in our Father's family. Many Christians fail in this area and as a result, their growth has been stunted.

And there was also a strife among them, which of them should be accounted the greatest.

And He said unto them, The kings of the Gentiles exercise lordship over them; and they that exercise authority upon them are called benefactors,

But ye shall not be so: but he that is greatest among you, let him be as the younger; and he that is chief, as he that doth serve. — Luke 22:24-26

In the original language, the word *younger* actually has a twofold meaning. It signifies *listening* and *learning!* Jesus's intent was to show us that a person who desires greatness must become a *listener* and a *learner*, not a talker or an egocentric know-it-all.

Jesus, Himself, was a listener. At the age of about 12, He was found in the temple asking questions of the elders and listening to them.

> *And it came to pass, that after three days they found Him in the temple, sitting in the midst of the doctors, both hearing them, and asking them questions.*
> *— Luke 2:46*

Listening is not a natural art. It must be practiced and cultivated. That's why St. Paul said, "Study to be quiet," and St. James exhorted, "Be quick to listen and slow to speak."

A brother once asked me, "Why is my ministry such a failure?" I didn't want to hurt him, but I felt obligated to be frank since he had asked.

"Brother so-and-so," I replied, "You are boring! Ninety-nine percent of the time you spend talking is about things that most of your listeners have no interest in whatsoever. You constantly talk about *your* problems, *your* hurts, *your* ambitions and *your* plans. When you learn to listen to others; their problems, their hurts, their ambitions, and their plans, then you will be successful."

I bought Brother so-and-so a little book that, in my opinion, is worth $60 million, but it only cost me 60¢. It was called, **How to Build Bridges to Other People**, by Clyde Narramore. That book revolutionized his ministry, and he's doing very well now that he has learned to be a listener instead of a constant talker.

Who Should We Listen To?

We should listen to people who have *genuine* problems and needs. I'm not talking about Sally SorryForMe or Cybil SympathySeeker. Those kind are professional time thieves. But I am saying we should listen to people who have real or perceived problems, as we look to God for words of wisdom to offer.

We should also listen to those who can teach us, even when they are considered by some to be intellectually unadvanced. The truth is, we can learn from every person we come in contact with, if we will only listen.

The wise man learns by listening ...
—Proverbs 21:11 TLB

The wise man is glad to be instructed, but a self-suffi-cient fool falls flat on his face.— Proverbs 10:8 TLB

Learning

In order to be learners, we must first be teach-able. Teachability is a real mark of intelligence. It is the quality of listening, learning, and translat-ing into everyday, practical living the truths and principles you've been taught.

The children of Israel wandered forty years in the wilderness because of their unteachable atti-tudes. It took forty years (1,364 times longer than it should have) to complete an eleven-day jour-ney! Perhaps you have faced the same trials over and over. The wilderness may be a familiar place for you. Well, don't go back again! *Learn* from your experience and don't repeat the same mistakes over and over again.

When people refuse to listen and learn, they forfeit their greatness.

Why Some Won't Listen And Learn

1. A feeling of self-importance. I remember a fellow who worked in a factory and would never accept any help or advice from anyone. One day he remarked, "If I ever quit, this factory would fall apart." He felt he had everyone over a barrel, so to speak. Well, he finally quit. That was several years ago and the factory still runs smoothly.

> *For I say, through the grace given unto me, to every man that is among you, not to think of himself more highly than he ought to think; but to think soberly, according as God hath dealt to every man the measure of faith.* — Romans 12:3

A junior officer was the engineer of the day aboard the U.S. Naval Ship Buck. He knew a little about a lot! After all, he was an officer of the United States Navy — a cut above ordinary enlisted men or so he thought. Well, one night while on duty, he yelled at the switchboard operator, "Close the bus tie circuit breaker!"

The sailor realized this would create serious consequences and responded, "But sir ...."

"I said, *close that bus tie breaker! That's a direct order!*" screeched the junior grade lieutenant.

"But sir, if I close that breaker, it will ...."

Just then the officer boldly ran to the front of the switchboard and closed the bus tie circuit breaker himself. The generators roared! The lights blinked and, slowly, all the ship's electrical power faded and eventually died. Radar equipment was ruined. The generators had to be rewired and thousands of dollars worth of damaged equipment had to be repaired. All of this happened because one proud officer would not listen to a man who knew what he was talking about. The enlisted man tried to tell the officer about the need to synchronize the A/C generator before closing the bus tie circuit breaker, but he wouldn't listen.

If only this young officer would have listened, he could have saved himself tremendous embarrassment.

... for God resisteth the proud, and giveth grace to the humble.   — *1 Peter 5:5*

Humble yourselves in the sight of the Lord, and he shall lift you up.   — *James 4:10*

2. Resentment of authority. Some will not listen and learn because they resent authority. Six millionaires in an affluent little church in the South resented the authority of their backwoods pastor, so they asked him to leave the church. But the pastor, knowing God had called him to that church, refused to go. So, instead, thinking the church could not survive without them, the millionaires left. They were wrong. That same church now has over 5,000 members and is a powerful influence in the entire nation. Nobody seems to know, however, what happened to those millionaires.

When a California pastor presented his God-given dream to his congregation, five of the church officers walked out, because they couldn't have things their own way. They resented the pastor's authority from God. They wanted to run the church their way. Well, today that church is known around the world. It has 10,000 members and great ministry teams that help hurting people daily. What about the five officers? Well, nobody seems to know what happened to them, either.

Korah, Datham, and Abiram resented Moses' authority and God's judgement speedily fell on them. But Jesus did not even resent Pilate's authority as governor, because He understood that unless God allowed him to, Pilate could have no power.

Then saith Pilate unto him, "Speakest thou not unto me? Knowest thou not that I have power to crucify thee, and have power to release thee?"

Jesus answered, "Thou couldest have no power at all against me, except it were given thee from above: therefore he that delivered me unto thee hath the greater sin."
— John 19:10-11

3. Wanting to do our own thing. An unteachable attitude can be a result of refusing to move in the flow of God's Spirit. It is the *me and Jesus got our own thing going* way of thinking. But what people with that philosophy are really saying is this: "I want to do my own thing. Don't bother me. I don't need Sunday School or church. Me and Jesus got our own thing going." Cain wanted to do his own thing, also. Because of it, he lived a life of failure.

Three associate ministers of a large church wanted to do their own thing. They announced to their following that they were breaking away from the mother church and starting a new church in town. They expected thousands to attend their new church. The senior pastor warned them, but they had heard from God for sure. What a shock they experienced when only a handful of people attended their new church. What a bigger shock when that handful returned to the mother church. Now all three of these former associate ministers are pastoring struggling, puny, little churches in their own unsuccessful efforts. Like Cain, they wanted to do their own thing and wouldn't accept wise counsel.

Thank God, He is raising up a group of people today who really mean business! People, like Enoch, who will walk *with* God. People who will listen, learn, and become more and more like Jesus every day!

*"And as the Spirit of
the Lord works within us,
we become more and
more like Him."*

— *2 Corinthians 3:18 TLB*

Chapter 7

Becoming Like Jesus

How does a believer become more like Jesus? Is there a plan, a divine blueprint? Can a person become like his Lord, or must he struggle through life constantly failing to live up to the example Jesus set? St. Paul was 30 years old in the Lord when he said:

> *I don't mean to say I am perfect. I haven't learned all I should even yet, but I keep working toward that day when I will finally be all that Christ saved me for and wants me to be.*

> *No, dear brothers, I am still not all I should be but I am bringing all my energies to bear on this one thing: Forgetting the past and looking forward to what lies ahead,*

> *I strain to reach the end of the race and receive the prize for which God is calling us up to heaven because of what Christ Jesus did for us.*

> *I hope all of you who are mature Christians will see eye-to-eye with me on these things.*
> — *Philippians 3:12-15a TLB*

Notice Paul said, "I haven't learned all I should even yet." Herein lies one of the keys to becoming like Jesus. After 30 years, Paul was more like Jesus than ever, but he humbly admitted there was still some work that needed to be done in his life.

As we listen and as we learn, we will *become!* Genuine learning, true education, will effect a change in our hearts, our lives, and our attitudes. As we listen to the Holy Spirit and learn from Him through the Bible and through God-anointed teachers of the Bible, we will find a gentle shaping of our lives taking place. God will be doing the work: no strain, no toil, no self-crucifixion.

> *And be not conformed to this world: but be ye transformed by the renewing of your mind, that ye may prove what is that good, and acceptable, and perfect, will of God.* — *Romans 12:2*

As we listen, learn, and renew our minds under the Lordship of Jesus Christ, we'll see ourselves becoming more and more like Him. Our problem is not really a spiritual problem once we have received Christ. Our real problem and stumbling block is the old, unrenewed, carnal mind. As that part of us is renewed with God's Word, the Holy Spirit will bring developments in our attitudes and character that will make us more and more like Jesus!

And as the Spirit of the Lord works within us, we become more and more like Him (Jesus).
— 2 Corinthians 3:18 TLB

Today, you and I are being conformed into one of two things: 1) the image of our Lord Jesus Christ or 2) something else. *What* you listen to and learn from and *who* you listen to and learn from will be a great factor in what you will become.

As an experiment, a farmer put a quart jar over a small pumpkin to see if it would grow. The pumpkin grew without any immediate squeeze. But after weeks of growth, the farmer discovered that the pumpkin grew no larger than the quart jar. He also observed it had grown to the exact shape of that jar! The jar determined the size and shape of the pumpkin. Many people are like that pumpkin. They are conformed by the world, or by a tradition, or by other people without realizing they are growing into the likeness of whatever they've allowed to shape them.

The television programs you watch, the books you read, the music you listen to, and the people you learn from, will determine where you will be (spiritually speaking) five years from now. You are being conformed! But, if the Holy Spirit is conforming you through God's Word, you can rest assured that the likeness of Christ is being produced in your life.

Rock Music

A war is raging! The world is battling to control our minds, endeavoring to bring us into conformity. Rocky Barra, former musician with the Beach Boys, and Stevie Wonder told me that one of the most dangerous things a person can do today is listen to secular rock music. Its lyrics program people's minds with words like:

> *The three men I admire the most,*
> *The Father, Son and Holy Ghost,*
> *They caught the last train for the coast ...*

When people hear songs like this, they register on their subconscious, and soon feelings of helplessness come over them. They become discouraged and don't know why. Subconsciously they feel that God is gone. He's not here anymore. He left for the coast! Although consciously they don't believe it is true, subconsciously (the part that aids in producing emotional feelings) they believe it, because *the subconscious mind cannot tell the difference between the truth and a lie!*

Many young people wonder why after being delivered from dope by Jesus Christ, they suddenly have an almost irresistible urge to go back on it. One reason is because of the music they listen to. A song about a trip on drugs was very popular some years ago:

> *Take me for a trip upon your*
> *Magic Swirling Ship*
> *My senses have been stripped*
> *And my hands too numb to grip!*
> *I promise to go anywhere with you.*

There was a time when songs about suicide were popular. Songs like *Patches, Alone Again,* and others like them. Today the suicide rate among teenagers is triple what it was ten years ago. Is it any wonder? Teens are subconsciously being conformed.

I received a call one night from a lady who was crying hysterically. "He's dead. He's dead," she cried. "D_____ is dead! He killed himself!" A young 17-year-old church member had joined a rock and roll group and got into the gloomy music in a heavy way. The devil conformed him and destroyed him.

Television

A president of a family-oriented broadcasting system stated that many of America's problems are the result of the wrong use of media by major networks.

For instance, the man who shot Ronald Reagan was inspired by the movie, *Taxi Driver.* He listened, he learned, he was conformed. I read that twenty-four young boys committed suicide playing Russian roulette after seeing the movie, *Deerhunter.*

One TV special showed some guys pouring gasoline over derelicts, igniting them, and watching them scream as they burned to death. After that program aired, dozens lost their lives when others used gasoline and fire to murder them on park benches in the slums.

The California Department of Education reported that high school seniors who watched six hours or more of television scored 14% lower in all areas than those who restricted their daily viewing to one hour or less.

Do you want to be like Jesus? Do you desire to be conformed into the image of someone or something else? Do you want your growth to be stunted like the pumpkin in a jar? Do you want your subconscious mind to be programmed by the world — or transformed by God?

As you *listen* and *learn*, you will *become*. Why not let your mind be transformed by the Bible, good Spirit-filled literature, wholesome Christian music, and inspiring, faith-building preachers? As you make this move, the Holy Spirit will make His move in making you more like Jesus, day by day.

"And whosoever shall compel thee to go a mile, go with him twain."

— *Matthew 5:41*

The Extra Mile

The person who consistently applies the Extra Mile Principle will never experience a shortage of open doors.

And whosoever shall compel thee to go a mile, go with him twain. — *Matthew 5:41*

At the time Jesus spoke those words, the law allowed any Roman soldier to compel a Jew to carry his military gear for one mile. But the soldier could not force anyone to labor in gear-handling more than one mile.

So then, what is Jesus saying here? He's saying this: *Do more than what's expected of you. Go another mile.* This is a real key to successful living. *Do more than what you're paid to do.* As we proceed in this chapter you'll see examples of people who applied this principle and reached high-level success as a result.

Mediocrity Mania

One of the saddest characteristics of today's society is the mania for mediocrity. People are satisfied to do just enough to get by and not one ounce more. "It's good enough for government work," is a common phrase. What a tragedy it is when a person settles for less than the best.

Because of this trend toward mediocrity, many people settle for mud pies when they could be baking cakes. Many build shacks when they could erect palaces and castles. Millions crawl when they could run. As Christians, we should be running — running the race to *win*, not to place second or third. Our goal should be to *win* and never settle for mediocrity. (Or as Jesus called it, lukewarmness. See 1 Corinthians 9:24, Revelation 3:15-16.)

How do we become winners? Simply by *getting in step* with the words of Jesus. When He spoke, He always spoke of keys that would help, promote, encourage, and lift us to new heights.

Elmer Wheeler, a famous American salesman, was sitting at the airport with Bill Patterson who was president of United Airlines at that time. Elmer made a remark, "Isn't it wonderful, Bill, how we finally conquered the air after all these years of trying?"

Bill responded, "Elmer, we never did conquer the air! That was our problem for all those flight-less years. We were trying to fight the air, conquer the air. When all along, all we had to do was to get in step with the principles — the laws — that were there all the time."

That's often our problem. We try to fight God's spiritual principles instead of getting in step with them. God's Word cannot be conquered. We cannot conquer spiritual laws. But we can get in step with those laws, and when we do, we'll find ourselves soaring like an eagle to new heights we never imagined.

If you haven't already, get in step today with the *"extra-mile law"*.

Bible People Who Applied The Extra-mile Law

Joseph didn't have to prayerfully plan to save Egypt from famine. After all, he was stuck in an Egyptian jail. But, he went the *extra mile* and speedily became the "vice president" of the nation.

Ezra was a teacher well learned in the Law and the King granted him everything he asked. Ezra was a teacher, not merely learned, but *well* learned. Because he was an *extra-miler*, he was rewarded by the king.

Hanani was chosen to be in charge of Jerusalem during the reconstruction of the wall because he was a man of integrity who feared God more than most men. Hanani received a powerful position because he was an *extra-miler.* (Nehemiah 7:2)

David's men were 100 to 1,000 times better than the average warriors, because they learned to shoot arrows with their left hands as well as their right. They went the *extra mile* in their preparation, and for 5% more effort, became 100 to 1,000 times greater. (1 Chronicles 12:2, 14)

The Extra Mile Is Often A Short Mile

Tom Landry, former coach for the Dallas Cowboys, was asked what the difference is between a pro and an all pro in the NFL. He responded by saying, "Not much. It takes a little more determination, a little more drive, a little more effort. It certainly is not ability, because many pros could be all-pros if they put forth 5% more effort." Imagine that! Try 5% harder and reap rewards that are 195% greater.

Anybody can do just what he or she has to do. But the real winner knows that a key to winning is going another mile. There is never any shortage of opportunities for the person who does a job consistently well, strives for quality, maintains a pleasant attitude, and gives just a little more than what is expected.

A young boy approached a construction supervisor with this question, "Sir, how can a guy become a foreman here?" The supervisor pointed and said, "Watch the fellow in the red shirt. Do what he does and you'll succeed. I've had my eye on him for several weeks now. Oh, he doesn't know I'm watching, but I am. He always does a little more than what he's paid to do. He has a great attitude toward his co-workers. While others are taking extra time for coffee breaks, he takes his break and is quickly back on the job. Next week I'm going to appoint a new foreman ... the guy in the red shirt!"

Ward Cameron

When Ward Cameron, a member of our church, was 84 years old, he and his wife, Sylvia, moved into an apartment complex for retirees and senior citizens. All that was expected of Ward was that he pay his rent. But because he was an *extra-miler*, Ward wasn't satisfied to sit back and do nothing. Soon Ward went to work on beautifying the grounds. He planted flowers, mowed the lawn, weeded the flower beds, shoveled the walks, and more, all on his own. He thought nobody noticed, and he didn't really care. As far as Ward was concerned, all the work he had done was *as unto the Lord*. But one day when Ward went to pay his rent, he was greeted with a message from the management. "Ward," a lady told him, "we have orders to cut your rent in half." Isn't that something? Rent was going up for everybody else, but Ward's went down!

Ward continued going the extra mile until they made him an official head of maintenance and completely quit charging him rent. Ward didn't stop there, however. He continued to go the extra mile, and eventually they paid him to stay in the building! He made himself so valuable by going the extra mile, the housing commission didn't want to lose him.

The extra mile always pays off! Anybody can be average, but why not be an extra-miler and enjoy the extra benefits?

"Not that I have already attained this, or have already been made perfect, but I press on to take hold of that for which Christ Jesus took hold of me."

— *Philippians 3:12 NIV*

Chapter 9

How To Be An Extra-miler

Why do only a few people bother to go the extra mile? I have found two reasons why the majority settle for mediocrity.

1. *They don't believe the words of Jesus.* True believing requires corresponding action. If a person really believes what Jesus said about the extra mile, they'll do it. Unbelief is usually expressed in rationalizations such as these:

- "My situation is different."

- "It won't work with my boss."

- "Only a fool does what he's not paid to do."

- "My husband? *Me* go the extra mile with him? Are you crazy?"

2. They don't look to the future; only to the "miserable" present. We think, "instant." We have instant coffee, instant oatmeal, instant hair conditioner, and instant printing shops. We want everything to happen NOW. "I'll go the extra mile once," some say, "and if it doesn't work, I'll go back to doing only what's expected." Then, without giving time for the seeds they've planted to grow, they go back to the old routine of just getting by. That's like plowing up a garden the day after planting the seeds. It is an immature attitude.

Many people even try to reap before they have sown. They try to harvest without planting. A farmer would be a fool to think that he could harvest a crop without planting much seed. And a person who expects to reap a harvest of benefits and rewards without planting seeds of excellence — *extra-mile seeds* — is a fool.

> *For whatsoever a man soweth, that shall he also reap.*
> — *Galatians 6:7*

> *But this I say, He which soweth sparingly shall reap also sparingly; and he which soweth bountifully shall reap also bountifully.* — *2 Corinthians 9:6*

How To Become An Extra-miler

1. *Believe there is great reward (both eternal and temporal)* for those who obey the words of Jesus. (Matthew 7:24-27)

2. *Make the decision to be an extra-miler.* Practice being an extra-miler at home, at work, everywhere! And don't be double-minded as to whether or not you want to apply this principle. (See James 1:8)

3. *Remember, the extra mile is often a short mile compared to the benefits that will be harvested.* I read of a young salesman who received an order for over a million dollars worth of furniture from one lady. All he did was give her a chair to sit on while she waited for the rain to stop. The young man did not know she was a multi-millionaire when she escaped the rain by coming into the department store. The other clerks ignored her, thinking she was just another window shopper. So who did she ask for when she wanted to furnish her castle? The extra-miler, of course.

A young bank executive received a new appointment with a sizable salary increase after he traveled the extra mile. The other junior executives thought it would be too much work to cover the duties of their colleague who left the bank unexpectedly. But the young *extra-miler* tackled the job effectively and efficiently. He also reaped a harvest of benefits.

The extra mile is often a short mile.

4. Personalize your work — do it "as unto the Lord." (Matthew 25:40; 1 Corinthians 10:23; Colossians 3:22-24.) In other words, do *God's* dishes, wash *God's* car, work for *God* no matter what you do. It's easier to work efficiently and go the extra mile for someone you love. Others can gripe and complain about the organization, but not you. *God is your boss!*

Do you want to see doors of opportunity open for you? Do you want to reap benefits like never before? Then *don't be satisfied with mediocrity! Be an extra-miler in your Father's family.*

God went the extra mile when He sent Jesus to die on the cross. He didn't send an angel or an animal. He went the *extra mile* and sent the very best — His only begotten Son.

Think of how many times God has gone the extra mile for you. Say "yes" to God today. Go the first mile by receiving Jesus Christ into your life. Go the second mile by planting extra-mile seeds of excellence in everything you do. A harvest of benefits and rewards awaits you! Pray this prayer right now:

Dear God,

I come to you in the Name of Jesus. Your Word says in John 6:37 that if I turn to You, You will in no way cast me out, but You will take me in, just as I am. I thank You, God, for that.

You also said in Romans 10:13 that if I call upon You, I'll be saved. I'm calling on You, Lord, so I know You have now saved me.

I believe Jesus died on the cross for me, and that He was raised from the dead. I now confess Him as my Lord.

I now have a new life. My sins are gone, and I have a new start, beginning NOW! Thank You, Lord!

Amen.

Published by

DECAPOLIS
PUBLISHING

For a catalog of products, call:

1-517-321-2780 or
1-800-888-7284

For Your Spiritual Growth

Here's the help you need for your spiritual journey. These books will encourage you, and give you guidance as you seek to draw close to Jesus, and learn of Him. Prepare yourself for fantastic growth!

SOMEBODY OUT THERE NEEDS YOU
Along with the gift of salvation comes the great privilege of spreading the gospel of Jesus Christ.

SEVEN SIGNPOSTS TO SPIRITUAL MATURITY
Examine your life to see where you are on the road to spiritual maturity.

THE PASTORS PAY
How much is your pastor worth? Who should set his pay? Discover the scriptural guidelines for paying your pastor.

THE DESIRES OF YOUR HEART
Yes, Jesus wants to give you the desires of your heart, and make them realities.

THE BEAUTY OF HOLINESS
Is holiness possible? Is it practical? How do you attain it? Find out how to pursue true holiness.

DECEPTION, DELUSION & DESTRUCTION
Recognize spiritual deception and unmask spiritual blindness.

These and other books available from Dave Williams and:

DECAPOLIS PUBLISHING

For Your Spiritual Growth

Here's the help you need for your spiritual journey. These books will encourage you, and give you guidance as you seek to draw close to Jesus and learn of Him. Prepare yourself for fantastic growth!

BE A HIGH PER-FORMANCE BELIEVER
Pour in the nine spiritual additives for real power in your Christian life.

SECRET OF POWER WITH GOD
Tap into the real power with God; the power of prayer. It will change your life!

THE NEW LIFE . . .
You can get off to a great start on your exciting life with Jesus! Prepare for something wonderful.

THE AIDS PLAGUE
Is there hope? Yes, but only Jesus can bring a total and lasting cure to AIDS.

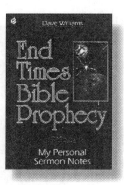

END TIMES BIBLE PROPHECY
Watch as events God spoke about thousands of years ago unfold to show us the nearness of Christ's return.

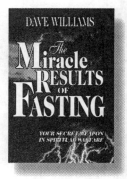

MIRACLE RESULTS OF FASTING
You can receive MIRACLE benefits, spiritually and physically, with this practical Christian discipline.

These and other books available from Dave Williams and:

DECAPOLIS PUBLISHING

For Your Spiritual Growth

Here's the help you need for your spiritual journey. These books will encourage you, and give you guidance as you seek to draw close to Jesus, and learn of Him. Prepare yourself for fantastic growth!

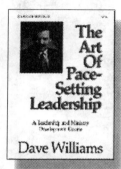

THE ART OF PACESETTING LEADERSHIP
Leaders are *made*, not born. You can become a successful leader with this proven leadership development course.

36 MINUTES WITH THE PASTOR
Join Dave Williams *this minute* for a daily dose of easy to understand devotions designed especially for you!

KNOW YOUR HEAVENLY FATHER
You can have a family relationship with your heavenly father. Learn how God cares for you.

SUPERNATURAL SOULWINNING
How will we reach our family, friends, and neighbors in this short time before Christ's return?

THE GRAND FINALE
What will happen in the days ahead just before Jesus' return? Will you be ready for the grand finale?

GENUINE PROSPERITY
Learn what it means to be truly prosperous! God gives us the power to get wealth!

These and other books available from Dave Williams and:

DECAPOLIS PUBLISHING

Expanding Your Faith

These exciting audio teaching series will help you to grow and mature in your walk with Christ. Get ready for amazing new adventures in faith!

ACRES OF DIAMONDS
Find your own acres of "diamonds" right where you are.

FORGIVENESS
The miracle remedy for many of life's problems is found in this basic key for living.

UNTANGLING YOUR TROUBLES
You can be a "trouble untangler" with the help of Jesus!

HOW TO BE A HIGH PERFORMANCE BELIEVER
Put in the nine spiritual additives to help run your race and get the prize!

BEING A DISCIPLE AND MAKING DISCIPLES
You can learn to be a "disciple maker" to almost anyone.

HOW TO HELP YOUR PASTOR & CHURCH SUCCEED
You can be an integral part of your church's & pastor's success.

These and other audio tapes available from Dave Williams and:

DECAPOLIS PUBLISHING

For Your Successful Life

These video cassettes will give you successful principles to apply to your whole life. Each a different topic, and each a fantastic teaching of how living by God's Word can give you total success!

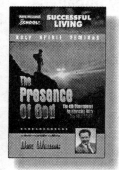

THE PRESENCE OF GOD
Find out how you can have a more dynamic relationship with the Holy Spirit.

FILLED WITH THE HOLY SPIRIT
You can rejoice and share with others in this wonderful experience of God.

HOW TO KNOW IF YOU'RE GOING TO HEAVEN
You can be sure of your eternal destination!

WHAT TO DO WHEN YOU'RE GOING THROUGH HELL
When you feel like you're going through hell, you have a choice to make.

A SPECIAL LADY
If you feel used and abused, this video will show you how you really are in the eyes of Jesus. You are special!

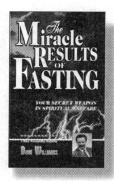

MIRACLE RESULTS OF FASTING
Fasting is your secret weapon in spiritual warfare. Learn how you'll benefit spiritually and physically! Six video messages.

These and other videos available from Dave Williams and:

DECAPOLIS PUBLISHING

Mount Hope Ministries

Mount Hope Missions & International Outreach
Care Ministries, Deaf Ministries & Support Groups
Access to Christ for the Physically Impaired
Community Outreach Ministries
Mount Hope Youth Ministries
Mount Hope Bible Training Institute
The Hope Store
The Pacesetter's Path Telecast
The Pastor's Minute Radio Broadcast
Mount Hope Children's Ministry
Sidewalk Sunday School
The Saturday Care Clinic

*When you're facing a struggle and need someone to pray with you, please call us at **(517) 321-CARE**. We have pastors on duty 24 hours a day. Or stop in Saturday between 11:00 AM and 1:00 PM for our walk-in care clinic. We know you hurt sometimes and need a pastor, a minister, or a prayer partner. There will be ministers and prayer partners here for you.*

If you'd like to write, we'd be honored to pray for you. Our address is:

West of the Lansing Mall,
on Creyts at Michigan Ave.

MOUNT HOPE CHURCH
202 S. CREYTS RD. LANSING, MI 48917
(517) 321-CARE or (517) 321-2780
FAX (517)321-6332 TDD (517) 321-8200

www.mounthopechurch.org